Through His Eyes –

What We Did To Overcome Depression

Linda Pearl Ramnath

And

Narendra Ramnath

Copyright © 2017 by Linda Pearl Ramnath

ISBN: Softcover – 978-0-9925761-2-7
ISBN: eBook – 978-1-3794730-3-1

All rights reserved. No part of this book may be reproduced or transmitted in any form or by any means, electronic or mechanical, including photocopying, recording, or by any information storage and retrieval system, without permission in writing from the copyright owner.

Rev. date: 02/09/2017

Unless otherwise stated, Scripture is taken from the Holy Bible, New King James Version® (NKJV), copyright © 1982 by Thomas Nelson, Inc. Used by permission. All rights reserved.

All other versions of The Holy Bible are taken from Biblehub.com. Copyright © 2004-2016 by Bible Hub. Used by permission
All rights reserved.

Published by Thy Soul Ministries

Acknowledgements

- ❖ We thank all our family and friends who supported us in the journey to finally put together this book. Your prayers have fueled our efforts to get this Sequel into other hands.

- ❖ Thank you to Sandy Nicholls, the artist who was so inspired by the first book, 'You Don't Have To Settle For Second Best! A Life Of Hope, Courage And Determination' that she painted the picture that appears on the cover page.

- ❖ We thank God for His strength and guidance in the whole process of recovery and renewal so that through our experience in dealing with depression, we could be a testimony for others searching for hope.

Contents

1. Introduction 7
2. Living with a person with severe depression 11
3. Reality check..12
4. Rage and madness...23
5. Despondency...27
6. There is no rule book 33
7. Father, take this cup … 36
8. Facing adversity...41
9. Man's best friend 45
10. Get out of the hole 48
11. Out of the closet..54
12. Courage 58
13. Have you ever suffered from depression?.....................62
14. Hope for the hopeless 65
15. Light at the end of the tunnel.......................................70
16. Changing adversity into advantage 77
17. Faith 80
18. Habits 85
19. Share it! 89
20. Concluding remarks 92
21. About the Author 94

Through His Eyes -

1. Introduction

Things can happen to anyone and sickness is no respecter of persons. What you least expect is oftentimes what happens. I never expected someone who is strong and intelligent to fall down and spiral into deep depression. When everything seems to be going well, tragedy strikes, like in the case of Job in the Bible. From being tired all the time and not able to finish tasks, the body soon caved in and I found my wife in a position where she could not help herself anymore.

Medication was the next step and the almost unending saga started for me. *I would leave in the morning for work and she was drugged, I came back and she was drugged to the eyeballs. There was no life! No life for her and certainly no life for me.* This dragged on for years and years. The side effects from the drugs she took caused thyroid imbalances which also caused significant weight gain.

Through His Eyes -

Sometimes there was a slight glimmer of hope but it was short-lived as my wife would have relapses. Anything could tip the balance for her and it was back to square one for everyone. As the years dragged on, my dear wife faded from life itself. She was almost impossible to live with most times. Sickness does that to a person; they lose that lacklustre for life. I was losing my wife and my companion and I didn't know what to do. Temptation was always there.

This book is about living with a person with severe depression. It looks at the seven-year journey of uncertainty and anguish in seeing someone who was vibrant and optimistic, sink into a pit of utter despair. During this seven-year period, I had to use all of my resources and energies just to stay on survival mode. My whole world changed and my outlook to life was severely compromised. My faith in God was tested time and time again. I just could not see any light at the end of this tunnel. Life became very meaningless. All my joy was gone and I had to live in an environment of emptiness and darkness.

Mental illness is very hard to classify and understand. Unlike a person on a wheelchair who you can see has a disability, mental illness is a hidden disability. In many cases the sufferer will make every effort to mask their symptoms from the public eye. I have learnt so much about mental illness and living with a person who was diagnosed with chronic depression that I felt I ought to share my experiences with others. Perhaps as you read my story you will learn something to help you cope with life if you have to support someone who is suffering from depression.

When someone you love is diagnosed with depression, you also suffer with them. In the attempt to help them, you can go off on the wrong path which can make the condition worse. This is what happened to me; when you are treading on thin ice, your emotional balance becomes severely affected. The mind can play tricks on you and you can end up in need of help yourself.
I have learnt that depression is not something to be ashamed of. Many people from all walks of life suffer with this crippling illness. If you try to handle it yourself,

you will burn yourself out. There is a lot of help for people suffering from depression and for their families. There is medical treatment and therapies of all sorts that can be accessed. Although depression is a debilitating illness, it can be treated effectively. Depression can be beaten!

In this book, 'Through His Eyes – What We Did To Overcome Depression' I share my most painful and intimate memories of living with my life partner through her long ordeal with severe depression.

2. Living with a person with severe depression

One of the most challenging things in my life was seeing someone 'dying' in front of me. Watching the light in their eyes slowly fading with each passing day was almost unbearable. I had so many questions... What did I do wrong? Why me? Why is she wasting her life like this? These questions did not lead me to answers. Instead it sent me on a guilt trip. This just made the situation worse.

The trauma and grief I experienced was similar to the death of a loved one. It was like going round and round the mountain. I often found myself crying in the bathroom. I felt so useless even though I was actively seeking help from different sources. Nothing I seemed to be doing was working.

I know that it doesn't pay to bottle things up. Sometimes you feel raging mad. Rage boils up inside and seeks an avenue for release. Subconsciously you may not realize how you are reacting to the madness around you. This is when you realize that even you can't do it alone and you are not the 'strong' one.

You do need help to cope with this heavy-laden situation. Counsellors can be most helpful at this stage. By receiving professional counselling, you are lightening your load because a burden shared is a burden halved. Most importantly, by looking up to God for His divine wisdom, protection and grace, you can successfully weather the storms of life.

3. Reality check

When sickness hits, it throws a curve ball at you. What you do with it determines what your life will be. Someone optimistically said that when live throws you lemons, you should make lemonade! So, take a moment to think about what *you* do in a bad situation!

Financial strain

When someone in your family is diagnosed with a chronic illness, you never know how long it is going to take for them to recover and sometimes big adjustments need to be made. In some cases, the person with a chronic illness never recovers. When you are used to living off two incomes and suddenly there is only one, big financial decisions need to be made. I found myself in a situation where doctors' bills and medication bills were mounting like an avalanche. Furthermore, travelling frequently to appointments with medical specialists caused a financial, physical and psychological strain on us.

I was exhausted all round and was operating on auto pilot. What else could I do? It was an unending battle with an invisible enemy. As time passed, the finances got stretched further and I contemplated selling our house. Fortunately, our eldest son started working and this helped us financially. My son also investigated

Income Protection and although it was not much, I found it to be very helpful.

The dreaded 'D' word

A few decades ago we all came to dread the 'C' word. Cancer and depression still leaves that gaping wound in the heart. Today, depression has become commonplace in our world. Questions that surface are: Why me? What did I do wrong? Why do I have to put up with this dreadful mental illness? The sufferer looks so normal to the outside world but they don't know the dark secret they are hiding.

I consider my most challenging life experience to be when my spouse had a career burn-out and fell into deep depression in 2009. *My world came crashing down, shattering all my dreams with it. I prayed and prayed but it seemed like all my prayers were ineffective.* She lapsed into a deep abyss. I found myself living with a stranger, a very hostile one too.

Even though it hurt so much, I still went to church because there was no plan B. *What pained me so much was to daily witness the sinking of an energetic, optimistic and intelligent friend. She was drowning and I couldn't save her, try as much as I did.* The pain was too much to bear but I knew I had to go on. Everyone was depending on me; my kids, my wife and my work. Life had thrown a black cloak over me. Still I must go on!

Mental illness is like a plague that consumes you from the inside. There was war some days in our household. When my wife went into her black moods, she would yell for no reason and would become violent and want to throw things around. She would not answer the phone or see anybody and would lock herself in her room. The children were terrified. I had to keep the peace between the boys and their mother.

Sometimes I thought I was witnessing a movie of the living dead. She was on heavy medication and walked around like a zombie. Sometimes I thought of putting her in a mental institution, but she refused outright. My intelligent wife would bark at me; she would repeatedly shout, 'My brains are cooked. I can never use my brains again.' Those statements pierced my heart deeply. To think that a gifted and talented person who lectured in English and Psychology would be reduced to this pitiful state, was too agonizing for me.

During that time, life for me was very lonely and scary, worse than a horror movie. Who could I confide in and where could I go? Very often when I was overwhelmed, I wanted to leave the house and chill out somewhere, but I never did. The Spirit within me kept reminding me that I must support my wife, no matter what. Finally, when we had exhausted all our resources, I decided to get my wife's mother to come from overseas to look after her for one year. Life was tough and we were all worn out!

In my quiet moments, I pleaded with God for answers. There was no light at the end of this tunnel. *My home was now a cold, dark house and I was imprisoned within its walls.*

Reasoning doesn't help and neither does complaining. Eventually I just surrendered to God and asked Him to give me the strength to go on. Strength was the most important thing I needed at that stage. My sanity was severely compromised and I had to put up with all the constant abuse from my delusional wife. There was no making sense of it. Only God knew what was going on in my head and in my home. I just had to trust Him to work it out somehow.

I took my ailing wife to the best doctors, psychologists and psychiatrists that I could afford. It was a very long and tiresome journey. She would be on such a low level of functioning that she was not even able to complete the battery of tests they administered to her. So, they medicated her even more. She just went deeper and deeper into herself. Very often she was not even there; her eyes were open but her soul was travelling to a distant place that no one could reach. She slept and slept, unaware of the world passing by her as days gave way to weeks, months and years. She just withered away, with no flicker of hope in her scaly eyes.

Through His Eyes -

Everybody knew how beautiful her soft green eyes were against her olive skin. Now all you saw was a shadow, a sallow frame without a flicker of light to meet your gaze.

The guilt trip

I always blamed myself for what went wrong. I said over and over to myself that I should have intervened in those early days. What went wrong and why did it have to happen to my family? I was the fighter, why not me? Why should she suffer because she is a lovely, calm person? I simply couldn't come to terms with all the injustice and the more I tried to make sense of it, the more confused and angry I became.

When things go terribly wrong, that is when you need added strength. I knew that there were many people praying for my family during this difficult time. I also knew that the best thing I could do for my family was not to carry that burden squarely on my shoulders. So, I cried to God to help me through those tough times.

One of the hardest things in life is to see someone so talented and successful being wasted away. Every day I felt so sad to see someone so powerful become so powerless. It was a bitter pill to swallow for me. Since their emotional state is very fragile, I found that you have to be very sensitive to the person suffering and just back off most of the time, just to keep the peace. So, in my soul searching I took to prayer and fasting and networked with prayer groups. *You need all the help you can get to keep your head above the water!*

The mother figure

The mother figure in the home is like a hub of a wheel; everything spins around her. When there is no mother in the home or when she is not able to function, everything is seriously affected. *With my wife being debilitated by her mental condition, her mother role was compromised and my kids were lost. We were not able to live; we were all just existing.*

Sadly, most people undervalue the role that mothers play. There is no use crying when they are gone if you do not respect and appreciate them when they are alive. I believe that God made mothers special; tender yet tough, patient and persevering and equipped with that special sixth sense. Mothers seem to know everything and you certainly cannot keep anything away from them. They are almost like blood hounds; they can smell a rat a mile away and this keeps the children in check too.

There was major malfunctioning in our home. Some of the family members were at loggerheads regarding the medical treatment my wife was receiving. Her symptoms varied from time to time. The black moods were really hard days and seeing someone become another person was hard to witness. Most people who knew her well, found my wife to be a level-headed person. That person was gone now!

There is no magic cure

There is no set time period for recovery when someone is suffering from depression. Sometimes they never recover at all. At first, I gave it three months thinking it was a work-related issue. Then six months passed and I thought the maximum time to recover would be one year. I never imagined it could stretch to seven long years.

We tried everything: alternate medication (which is good but very expensive), massage therapy (head massage was helpful) and holiday breaks, to name a few. Our friend would cook some meals, coerce my wife out of the bed and try to get her out of the house. The family would always try to go out to some place, away from the stress and strain of the home. The boys tried their best but unfortunately, their mother remembered very little of it as she was in her own world.

Support structures are vital to the sufferer's recovery as well as for the sanity of the family. *Spiritual support from godly people, emotional support from family and friends and medical support from the medical team is most important and should never be underestimated.* Although there is no magic cure, the combined efforts of all team players can significantly contribute to the recovery of the person suffering from depression. We found that depression can be beaten!

4. Rage and madness

When you learn that your loved one has a mental illness, rage can build up inside you like a deep well of bitter water. *The one thing I have learnt very slowly and painfully was not to keep all those negative feelings inside. Take my advice; you definitely should not bottle up all those ill feelings. It can fester inside your mind like a hornet's nest and drive you crazy.* You certainly don't need to inherit the madness of the illness as well. Therefore, I caution you to think smart and act smart! Believe me, it is a case of 'been there, done that.'

When a person has depression, one of the first warning signs you will notice is the disturbance in their sleep patterns. I noticed excessive sleep patterns initially which was followed by very bad insomnia. My ailing wife was so tired she could barely keep her eyes open when she got back from work. It was a miracle how she managed to cook the evening meal each night. I suppose she was operating on auto pilot. She always put the children and myself ahead of her needs and no matter what, she made sure they did not go to bed on an empty stomach.

It seemed like there were two things on her agenda each day: go to work and feed the kids, then CRASH! Lights out for her, no communication whatsoever! I don't think she ever heard a word I said. It was like her brain was on reserve tank, bordering on depletion, ready to shut off.

Then I found I could not get her to wake up each morning to go to work. Her body just flopped; it could not make it. She simply ran out of steam like an overworked locomotive train. She just lay there on the bed in a pathetic heap. *There was nothing I could say or do. I was hopelessly abandoned and I never felt so terribly frightened and helpless.*

We all faded into oblivion for my wife. Nothing mattered, nobody mattered. I wonder if she knew whether she was alive or walking dead. Food, children, work – what are those things? She was drifting, far away from us, far from this world – like a mist, the advancing fog consumed her. I think we lost her for days on end. She was there but not with us. How much more frightening it must be for young minds who barely grasp this new 'sickness' their mother had. The thing is, when you yourself don't understand what is happening, how do you explain it to your young children?

So, I knew I needed to seek help; medical help for a start. It was quite obvious to the medical practitioner that this was a classic case of depression. 'Take 3 pills; one in the morning, one at lunch and one at night and see me in 2 weeks' time', they told us. Then the 'fun' began; weeks turned to months and months rolled into years. Yes, there were checks and balances but it seemed like we were just buying a huge roll of band aids. Addressing the symptoms is no way to get to the underlying cause of it.

From sleeping too much my poor wife went to not sleeping at all. All night long she roamed about the house, pacing up and down, doing 'stuff'. She was always tired and always thinking. She needed time to 'think'. It was hard to believe there was an intelligent person inside that body. She was doing insane things like adjusting picture frames or swapping them around all the time. Everything had to be changed; furniture got moved (by herself, strangely), plants got moved, everything got a new place. Sometimes I would come home and think I was in the wrong house. Insanity was reigning supreme in this house!

When you are sleep deprived, anything out of the ordinary can happen. She started seeing things and hearing voices. The house was bewitched, she would say. Yet nobody else could see or hear anything strange. Perhaps there was something wrong with us, she would say. Madness and rage were slowly becoming the order of the day. How could we live another day like this?

When you think, things could not get any worse, how come they just do? So, it was sleep all day and awake all night. Next it was walk around the neighbourhood in the midnight hours. This was too much for us! We were in crisis mode! I needed help and I needed it real fast! If something didn't change real soon, I knew I was going to crack!

A lifeline is the source you rely on when you have depleted all your resources. I had to use a lifeline to save a life. In fact, not just one life; all our lives were hanging on the balance now. My kids were scared of their own mother. That's when Granny came to live with us. She was our last resort. Our ship was sinking real fast!

5. Despondency

When faith is all but gone, we have a foreboding sense of despondency. No matter how much we try, there is that sadness, gloom and disillusionment that permeates our entire being. In our misery, we feel dejected by the whole world and our downcast soul despairs even more. Oftentimes, nothing others say to us can lift us from our downheartedness. We find ourselves sinking into a deep hole. This is a very cold and lonely place to find yourself in.

What do you do when the odds are stacked up against you? Hebrews 11:1 is a solid pointer to the rope we need to grab when we are sinking fast. It says, "Now faith is the substance of things hoped for, the evidence of things not seen." It is only through the eyes of faith and not our literal eyes, that we are able to understand things. Faith enables us to not only understand the situation better but gives us a life line to grasp so we can receive the strength to survive the ordeal we are going through.

King David was a man who knew suffering first hand. In Psalm 88 he prays a prayer for help in his state of great despondency. Verse 1 opens with the lines, "O Lord, God of my salvation, I have cried day and night before You." In the midst of his intense grief he still acknowledges God as the God of his 'salvation' because He realizes that his only hope comes from God Himself.

As the psalm progresses we read of the state of his vexed heart. Verses 9-11 show his anguish;
"My eye mourns by reason of affliction: LORD, I have called daily upon you, I have stretched out my hands unto you. Will you show wonders to the dead? shall the dead arise and praise you? Shall your lovingkindness be declared in the grave? or your faithfulness in destruction?" Even in the darkest hour, we see a faith so strongly rooted that it grasps hope for the hopeless. King David asks, 'Will You work wonders for the dead?' This shows us that he knows the majestic power of God and still holds onto hope because of it.

God is indeed faithful. He is unchanging; no situation of ours, no matter how bleak it may appear to us, is insurmountable for Him. He holds the whole world in His hand. All we have to do is like King David; put our full trust in Him. Hebrews 12:2 (NASB) says, "fixing our eyes on Jesus, the author and perfecter of faith, who for the joy set before Him endured the cross, despising the shame, and has sat down at the right hand of the throne of God." Our Lord Jesus overcame and I held on to this same assurance that I too will overcome as my family and I fully commit our lives to the Lord's capable leading.

I shudder to think what it would have been like if I could not go personally to God in prayer and lay my case before Him. In our own strength, we can do nothing. We get depleted faster than we can anticipate. Our resources are very limited and there is no guarantee that what we are doing is going to work out just fine because we certainly do not know the future. I thank God that although I cannot predict the future, I can go to Him with the full assurance that He is ever present and all knowing. Therefore, I can lay my heavy load and ask Him to carry me on this part of my journey.

When you come to that realization that God has you all figured out and your welfare is safe in His hands, you can look at your situation from a different perspective. You do not need to feel overwhelmed because you are no longer carrying that burden alone. Although things may not have changed dramatically in your situation, you get that inner peace that all is well. It is at this stage that your soul rests in the divine assurance as you rely on the providence of God to see you through.

People who have not been at the helm of adversity may think you are in denial. It is only those who have walked where you walk and have drunk of the bitter cup of despondency, who know exactly what you are talking about. Remember, a sword is formed by being flaked several times on a hard rock. It needs to undergo that process for it to become an effective weapon of combat.

Through His Eyes -

As a child of God, we need to realize that He knows what we are going through and also how much we can endure. His grace is sufficient for us and His power is made perfect in our weakness (2 Corinthians 12:9). Just as no earthly father will make his child carry a suitcase that is too heavy for him, our Heavenly Father knows what we can bear and in His time, He comes to our rescue. Psalm 88:12 asks the questions, "Shall Your wonders be known in the dark? And Your righteousness in the land of forgetfulness?" Suffice it to say, God is Faithful. Dear reader, I believe you will vicariously experience this reality when you get to the end of this book.

6. There is no rule book

Where do you turn to when someone you love is losing themselves? There is such a stigma attached to mental illness and depression that very often the sufferer and his family are afraid to tell others. Sometimes they may not want to seek medical or psychological help because they do not want to be labelled. Yes, it is true that your chances of prospective work will be sharply curtailed when you say that you have had a mental condition. Nobody wants to take that risk of employing someone who might relapse into their mental condition, given the slightest provocation.

What is the right thing to do when faced with this mental illness? Obviously when someone has a physical ailment, they do not hesitate to visit a doctor. When they have a dental problem, it doesn't matter how long they have to wait to get an appointment, people do not think twice about seeing a dentist. So why are people generally so reluctant to seek medical help for a mental condition? Do the right thing and get a medical opinion when your loved one manifest signs of despair and gets depressed easily. Their body is showing you that they are not coping with the situation they find themselves in.

Sadly, there is no rule book offering a guide on how to go about handling a person with depression symptoms. That is because there is no 'one size fits all' solution to the problem. There are so many things on the market offering treatment for depression. How do you know which is the right pathway for your loved one? One thing is sure; there is no quick fix solution for depression.

In my experience in helping my wife get out of her state of depression, I have been careful to observe her reactions over time. Sometimes some medication is just not suitable for the person and instead of helping them, it simply masks the symptoms. I have found that you need to go by your 'instinct' if you wish to make progress with this medical illness. Since you live with the person 24/7, you are the best person to know exactly how they are doing.

Look for the signs and go by your instinct. However, one word of caution here; don't let the sick person pull the wool over your eyes. I have found that cover up is one of their biggest defenses. They do need help because they have exhausted their resources to cope. Otherwise they would not be in the mental state they find themselves in. So please remember, this is definitely not the time to keep silent. If you think of it as though you are fighting an enemy of the mind, you won't keep silent.

Procrastination is the thief of time. The more we put off seeking help, the bigger the problem is going to become. You simply cannot 'wish' it away or use the 'wait and see' approach. Help is available, so reach out for it from the onset. If you do nothing, the sufferer will sink deeper and deeper into that black hole of despair. *I have found that a combination of medical intervention, counselling, group therapy and spiritual support have worked wonders in addressing the root cause of the mental issue.* Additionally, the support of family is vital to the healing process. It is said that a family that prays together, stays together. Everybody needs to do their part in helping the sufferer deal with the situation rather than each hiding from it. There is certainly no rule book to turn to but a concerted effort from all parties concerned will help alleviate a lot of stress and tension for everyone living with the sufferer.

7. Father, take this cup ...

Why should the innocent suffer? There are so much bad things that many people do yet it seems in the majority of cases their crimes go unpunished. If they do pay for it, very often the sentence does not fit the crime because humanitarianism overrides the better judgement of people. So, crime goes on unabated and in fact exacerbates with each new generation. Many people who end up with depression have invariably been victims of circumstances. It could be a worker who is bullied by his boss, a spouse who is manipulated in her marriage relationship, a mother who has just lost a child, a student who has failed an exam and the list goes on and on.

Why do bad things happen to good people? There is no clear-cut answer to that question and in some cases, we will never know. Only God knows and when things don't make sense to us, all we can do and *should do* is take it to Him in prayer. This is the time we should run 'to' God rather than run 'away' from Him, as is the case with many people who become so disillusioned with the situation they find themselves in.

Indeed, when we don't know what to do, we can go to God who is our Heavenly Father and humbly ask Him, 'Father will You please take this cup (of bitter uncertainty) from me?' Next, you have to exercise that child-like faith and totally rely on Him to handle your affairs from that moment on. I know as humans this is not an easy thing to do, especially when you don't get a response immediately. But when you are walking that tightrope blindfolded, all the distractions in this world don't matter. You know you have to get to that other side so you muster all the inner strength you have and concentrate on what you have to do. This is called 'blind faith'; you don't see the outcome yet you know deep down in your heart you are going to make it.

In all things we go through in this life, we are instructed to give thanks (1 Thessalonians 5:18). Why should we do this? The latter part of this verse qualifies it with the words "for this is the will of God in Christ Jesus concerning you." When we subject our will to the will of God we come to that stage where we 'quite' our spirit. We shut out all the distracting thoughts that threaten to flood our minds and we fix our gaze fully on Christ Jesus. Hebrews 12:1-2a says, "Therefore we also, since we are surrounded by so great a cloud of witnesses, let us lay aside every weight, and the sin which so easily ensnares us, and let us run with endurance the race that is set before us, looking unto Jesus, the author and finisher of our faith…" How uplifting is that! We need to give thanks always even if it does not make sense to us at that time.

In the stillness, He speaks. When we place ourselves in a position where we can focus on the things that really matter, we look at things for what they really are. It is like when we have removed all the dirt that is around the gold only then will we be able to see the beauty of that gold nugget. In Psalm 46:10 the Psalmist writes, "Be still, and know that I am God: I will be exalted among the nations, I will be exalted in the earth." We are able to source His Power and allow it to infuse our bleak situation. This is the point where we get supernatural intervention into our lives.

Have you noticed especially in wealthy people, how they are so full of wealth yet so empty in their souls? When we come to the point of spiritual reawakening, we are filled within our soul. That yearning and void within us dissipates and we position ourselves to partner with the Holy Spirit. Only then are our batteries supercharged and we are reconnected and empowered to face life and its challenges.

We do not have to despair when we put our full trust in God. He knows the situation we are in and He is faithful to see us come out of it when we commit it to Him. 1 Peter 5:6 (NIV) says, "Humble yourselves, therefore, under God's mighty hand, that He may lift you up in due time."

When we go to our Heavenly Father and say, 'Father, take this cup from me', He sees our pain, hears our cry and answers us in His time. The enemy of our soul has one sole purpose; to rob us of the goodness that God has in store for us. He is a liar, a deceiver and the destroyer of all that is good and pleasant in the sight of God. But rest assured, God has us covered and He will restore unto us up to seven times over. He is constant and His love for us is unfaltering. Just trust Him to work it all out perfectly because this is in keeping with His nature.

8. Facing adversity

When adversity comes our way, sometimes the best thing to do is to dig our heels deep into the ground and stand firm! Life is tough; we need to get used to it! There is a saying, 'when life gets tough, the tough get going!' So there comes a time in our lives when we simply have to bite the bullet and face life! Unfortunately, many people are like ostriches; they bury their heads in the dirt and wish their situation would go away. This approach does not work, unless of course you are an ostrich.

I know it is easier said than done and when you are bogged down with your situations, the last thing you think of is fighting it. I have often found myself in such situations where I felt I just wanted to quit. But then I remembered the WWJD test (What Would Jesus Do). So, I would ask myself: 'What would Jesus do if He was in my situation? Jesus always listened to our Heavenly Father and Matthew 26:39 records, "He went a little farther and fell on his face, and prayed, saying, 'O My

Father, if it is possible, let this cup pass from me; nevertheless, not as I will, but as You will.'"

When we were at a marriage course, the speaker reminded us of a simple principle: 'The best thing to do for our children is to love their mother!' This is the essence of demonstrating a Christ-like love to someone who is most unlovable. It takes strength and courage to shower love to a person who is constantly attacking you. But this is what we are commanded to do. In season and out of season, our love should be constant to our partners.

When you are constantly facing adversity, which voice do you listen to? The voice of emotion shouts loudly and requires justice. You know you are being treated badly and you know you don't deserve such treatment. When you look at the situation, everything within you says, 'This is not right; I don't need to put up with it.' On the other hand, the voice of the Holy Spirit speaks directly into our spirit. We know that the Holy Spirit is seen as our 'helper' and is there to guide us in the path of truth and righteousness. John 14:26 (ESV) says, "But the Helper, the Holy Spirit, whom the Father will send in my name, he will teach you all things and bring to your remembrance all that I have said to you." We have to think very carefully about whose voice we want to appease when we are facing situations of adversity. The choice is ours and we have to live with the consequences of our decision.

Since love covers a multitude of sins, we need to forgive and release the person who has wronged us. We don't know what is going on inside their heads. We should not even attempt to play God. What we do know is obedience is better than sacrifice and sacrifice comes with a huge price tag. When God commanded us husbands to love our wives in Ephesians 5:25, it was a command. It was not based on situations. We are to love them in good times and bad times, even when we are feeling overwhelmed in the face of adversity. *I must confess, the thought to leave my ailing wife did cross my head but then I remembered that I had made a vow to her in marriage that I would be with her through good times and bad times. So, that settled it and I could not go back on my word.*

If you have a moment of hesitancy on the way you should go, read John 14:15-16 (ESV) where it says, "If you love me, you will keep my commandments. And I will ask the Father, and he will give you another Helper, to be with you forever." When you turn your attention to God and ask Him to help you deal with the adverse situations you are facing, you receive His peace. He knows the past, present and future and who better to look up to than such a great source.

Philippines 4:7 (NIV) says, "And the peace of God, which transcends all understanding, will guard your hearts and your minds in Christ Jesus." Our Lord Jesus Christ knew exactly what we experience and how troubled our hearts can become because He lived here on earth and saw first-hand the turmoil that often surrounds us. The peace He is talking about is out of this world and can only be enjoyed as we accept His Lordship into our lives. We are never alone and we don't need to worry or be afraid of the situations we face. As He has overcome, we too will overcome. We have a friend that sticks closer to us than a brother. What a reassurance!

9. Man's best friend

Everybody needs a friend. I have never been a great dog lover when I was a child because I was bitten by a dog. When I first got a puppy for my children, I grew to love the pet so much as it brought us so much joy. These animals give so much yet ask so little in return. I have found that pets can also be a great source of stress relief.

They say that no man is an island. Although we are born with different temperaments and grow up to form our unique personalities, we are people who need others. We emotionally impact others and even animals can sense our emotions. A dog can sense whether you are afraid of it or not. Many tradespeople will tell you that a dog is a very reliable and loyal friend to man, especially when you have to travel long distances to a job.

Through His Eyes -

A person with depression functions on a lower affective level than others. Their emotions and feelings have reached an ebb tide. Their passion for life is almost gone and there is no excitement in their lives. They look as if their batteries have gone flat. Our normal reaction is to help them recharge those batteries. This is the condition I found my dear wife in and very often I could not reach her. Where do we find a friend who is faithful, consistent, patient and non-judgmental?

Although people generally have the best intentions, unless they are a mental health professional, they cannot rightly help the person suffering with depression. The reason is that very often our 'affect' gets in the way. We do not want to see the sufferer in that state and we try everything we can to motivate them to get out of it. We are tempted to rationalize the situation and try to sermonize them. When that strategy fails, we try other means, most of them in verbal form. What tends to happen is the sufferer cannot absorb so much and switches off. We end up getting frustrated and discouraged ourselves. This is what happened in my situation when I tried to help my wife the best I could but I was so wrong.

Even the person suffering with depression needs a friend. They need someone who will accept them as they are and would not react to their situation. They need someone who will stick with them through thick and thin. That's where man's best friend comes to the rescue. They say that a dog is man's best friend for a justifiable reason. Notice how a dog starts wagging its tail to welcome you even when you are a long distance from it. Many dogs will run up to you eagerly for a little pat on their head.

When you are relaxing after a hard day, you know for sure that your dog will not burden you with its own problems. What a loyal friend to have! So, it is not surprising that a person with depression will slowly warm up to a dog as a pet. I discovered that when my son bought his first dog, she was just 5 weeks old and she worked her magic around us. Even my wife in her depressed state, warmed up to this little furry bundle of joy. A thin smile would appear on her face which developed into an occasional laugh when this fluff ball would try to lick her face. How amazing and how therapeutic are pets!

There are many dog movies that have become box office hits. These include: Lassie, The Red Dog, Beethoven, One Hundred and One Dalmatians and the list goes on. Dog story books that are well worth reading are Jock of the Bushveld and White Fang. We can learn so many lessons from man's best friend. Can you imagine a world without our beloved pets? They certainly provide us with a lesson on unconditional love!

10. Get out of the hole

The hole is the pit we fall into. It can become a deep abyss for the soul where it is fenced by darkness, coldness and despair. This great void causes emptiness in the soul that makes life fearful, meaningless and relentlessly painful. This is definitely not the place for anyone to be in.

When you find someone has fallen into the hole, you want to help them get out of it. You need to be a source of help to the sufferer to enable them to get out of the hole. Most importantly, they need to get out of the environment they are stuck in. Very often they would resort to the comfort of their house or even their own room. This is the place they can hide in unnoticed as the world goes by. *I have found that sitting there and 'counselling' the sick person is not going to help. You are not the expert!* So, get out of the house and get help for your loved one and for yourself. If you don't, you could find yourself treading on thin ice.

We know that the sun is our primary source of life. It is our vital source of vitamin D from which the body is able to draw important nutrients to combat the harmful substances in our environment. When there is an absence of light, productivity comes to a grinding halt. The creative juices in a person starts to dry up and they have to draw from their reserve tank to operate on survival mode from day to day. This is a dangerous state to be in because the body needs a certain amount of fluids, nutrients and chemicals to operate within a normal level of functioning. Chemical deprivation can result in chemical imbalance which in turn can adversely affect the functioning of the whole body.

Nature offers healing and restoration. Although the sufferer may feel so low and demotivated, burying themselves under the covers of their bed linen is not going to help in any way. You need to lovingly support and encourage them to get out into the sunshine. That is where we draw our source of life, light and energy. This place helps us recharge our batteries!

Nature is beauty at its best! It is incomparable to any man-made creation. Nature is not static; it is living and life giving. There are more negative ions in the atmosphere in forests and near moving water. These oxygen ions reduce stress levels and improve overall mood and boost serotonin levels. When your loved one is sick, take them on a walk and see what happens. They need that exercise to reduce cortisol, the stress hormone. A person cannot remain unchanged after being out in nature because this is such an invigorating force. *I have found that being out in nature and getting some sunlight has positively charged my depressed wife's body and soul.*

Just watching the flowers, the trees and the birds is in itself very therapeutic. Looking at the streams of fresh flowing water from the mountain creek is so appeasing to the eye. Listening to the water cascading down the rocks is soothing to the mind. Subconsciously we are invigorating our spirits and refreshing our souls. That deep void within our souls becomes filled with lively images that leave a soothing experience in the mind's eye. As we are drenched by the beauty of nature, we experience a quenching which fills us, revives us and simultaneously restores us to wholeness.

There is great power in nature, much greater than the average person gives it credit. Look at the waves of the sea – observe the ebb and flow of the tide and the synchronism of its movement. Look at the beauty of a flower bud as it raises its head to the light – watch as it mechanically opens up each outer petal to embrace the atmosphere and adorn the environment. Look at how the rain clouds gather and lower in the atmosphere as they gravitate towards the parched earth. Look at the darts of electric energy as the lightning flashes across the stormy sky. Nature is paradoxically a beautiful and perilous force.

Nature is for man's healing as well. If we want to get out of that hole that depression can push us into, we need to focus on a positive source to renew us. The question is: how do we tap into nature and direct its energy into our human spirit? Matthew 6:26 (NIV) says, "Look at the birds of the air; they do not sow or reap or store away in barns, and yet your heavenly Father feeds them. Are you not much more valuable than they?" Nature exists because it was created by our Heavenly Father. Therefore, isn't it a logical deduction that we need to acknowledge Him, the Creator of the universe, as our source of help?

I have found that nature and nurture are two important elements for addressing mental health issues that threatens the balance and harmony of a home. While people try their best to take care of the person who is sick, they should never underestimate the power of nature. I see nature and nurture as two sides of a coin. You can't have the one without the other. Allow me to illustrate; after being cooped up indoors during a week of rain, the sun comes out on the weekend. What do you do? Naturally, people head outdoors to the beach or parks or go for a long drive somewhere. When they return from their adventures, they feel relaxed and invigorated. Why? It is the healing power of nature at work. How amazing!

Whenever opportunity lent itself, I would take my ailing wife out to the mountains or the rainforests. She loves walking and seeing new places. Out in the open, she was a different person; her eyes would widen with child-like curiosity to see some lizard scramble along the walking trails. She would gaze at the wild vines that intertwined the tall trees in the forest, lost in wonder and amazement. The look on her face during those times was priceless. It was hard to believe she was sick at all during such moments. Nature certainly has that special way of renewing the soul.

11. Out of the closet

There are some words that people like to keep hidden. They are afraid that if they use them, people would think they are weird and not mentally stable. Depression is one of those words but the truth is, the better you understand the illness, the less scared you will be of it. Ignorance is no excuse for evading issues. When someone has depression, there are other words that come with it like anxiety, panic attacks, mania, hallucinations, post-traumatic stress disorder, manic, psychotic episodes and the like.

Generally speaking, when you are tired, your anxiety goes up. The ability of your body and mind to cope with the stressful situation is drastically reduced and the adrenal glands go into overdrive. Anxiety can be caused through environmental or genetic factors. Stressors within the environmental could range from the loss of a job, flooding, fires or any potentially harmful situation. There are also psychological factors such as war or personal trauma that can bring a person to 'rock bottom'. Those who come from families where mental health issues plague the generations are more susceptible to depression than others. So, when you go to the doctor on stress related issues, they often ask about family history.

In most cases, warning signs of a mental meltdown are so subtle that people don't notice them. Very often the sufferer doesn't notice it himself at first. What I observed in my wife was oversleeping; I couldn't believe that a person could sleep so much and still be tired. Although she was sleeping a lot, I later realized that her mind was actually working on overdrive. She was always thinking and thinking, like a wound-up clock that wouldn't stop ringing. This is probably why depressed people are always tired.

The opposite of oversleeping is insomnia and in some cases the two can get switched around, like in my wife's case. She would be up all night and constantly changing things around the house when everyone was asleep. She had that restless energy that would often drive the rest of us crazy. Instead of doing something constructive, she would repeatedly engage in meaningless activities. She was never settled and this was unsettling for the rest of us. I never knew where to find things because they were moved around so often and this stressed me out even further. Insomnia ruins your health and robs you of your time. It is like carrying a sack of potatoes over your shoulders every single day; it weighs you down.

In all those trying years I often found myself feeling guilty. I thought of what could have been the situation if I had taken notice of the warning signs. I kept on going over scenarios in my mind and the more I thought things over, the more confused I became. *I was angry with myself and sometimes angry with God. I finally came to a realization that I could not do things in my own strength.* I realized that we don't have to carry those heavy burdens. Matthew 11:28 (NLT) says, "Then Jesus said, "Come to me, all of you who are weary and carry heavy burdens, and I will give you rest." What a relief and what a comfort that was for me. I wept before God and asked Him to help me. I didn't need to hide the reality of my wife's sickness from the rest of the world and I certainly didn't need to shoulder all that responsibility.

When you are preoccupied with yourself and your situation, you start to feel sorry for yourself. This is not what God wants for you; He wants you to be in good health and prosper. When you come to the Lord, you will find that there is healing in His hands. I knew that I had to stop that 'stinking thinking' because it was leading me towards a dung hill. 3 John 1:2 (NIV) says, "Dear friend, I pray that you may enjoy good health and that all may go well with you, even as your soul is getting along well." *I found that I had to align my thinking to what God planned for my life and the life of each member of my family.* We need to make this a daily habit so that we will be renewed in our souls and refreshed in our bodies.

It is no surprise that there were many clinically depressed people who were really successful in their lives. You simply have to do a google search and you will be amazed how common depression is amongst even rich and famous people. Some of the great men in history who battled depression include Lincoln, Churchill and Hemmingway. What surprised me even more was when I discovered that they were great people not in spite of their condition but *because* of their condition. This is certainly something to think about!

12. Courage

Courage is a vital part of our lives because without it we will not be able to face life's day-to-day challenges. To have that courage, we need to have determination that no matter what life throws at us, we will not take it sitting down. When we determine in our mind that we are going to move forward, nothing can stop us. It is that inner strength to persevere against all odds that will see us through the difficult times in our lives. Some people call it 'intestinal fortitude' which is a nice way of looking at it. The opposite of courage is feebleness or faintness. Who wants to be called feeble?

It goes without saying that not every season in our lives will be a season of happiness. There are times of trials and times of great hardship but they are just seasons in life, just like the four seasons in the year. *The important principle I have learnt is that no matter what season I go through in life, I know that God is right there with me.* Even in the winter season, we should not despair because we know that spring is coming around the corner. We just need to hold firm on the promises of God. Why should we lack courage and become despondent when winter comes in our lives?

Timing is everything; ask a farmer, a pharmacist, a racing car driver and they will all tell you how important it is to get the timing right. Psalm 126:5 (NIV) says, "Those who sow with tears will reap with songs of joy." As long as you know that you are going through a season, you can anticipate the day when that bad season changes for the better. *I always dreamed of re-experiencing the good days with my wife. Deep down in my heart I yearned to see her celebrate life's simple pleasures with me once again.* When I looked at her in her depressed state, it seemed like wishful thinking but then I looked to God's promises and that gave me the courage to stay focused and move on.

If we find ourselves fainthearted in the midst of great trials, we should remember that God has promised us strength and power. In 2 Corinthians 12:9 (NIV) we read, "But he said to me, 'My grace is sufficient for you, for my power is made perfect in weakness.' Therefore, I will boast all the more gladly about my weaknesses, so that Christ's power may rest on me." We find here that the Apostle Paul was inundated with trials but it didn't faze him because he knew where his strength came from. Likewise, we don't need to become the victims of our circumstances. When we have the courage and boldness that God gives us, we can rise from our circumstances as victors of 'conquests'. This is an advantage position, being in the 'offence' mode rather than being in the 'defense' mode.

When we have God on our side, we are definitely on our way to victory. In 2 Corinthians 10:4 (NIV) it says: "The weapons we fight with are not the weapons of the world. On the contrary, they have divine power to demolish strongholds." For our part, we simply need to take on that child-like faith and trust God to work everything out in our favour. In this way, He is glorified because we have surrendered our agenda to His divine plan. For me, this was a long and hard lesson to learn but I eventually came to that point of realization and totally put my trust in God. Isaiah 12:2 (NIV) says, "Surely God is my salvation; I will trust and not be afraid. The LORD, the LORD himself, is my strength and my defense; he has become my salvation."

Courage is trusting God and not being afraid. When you come to that part of your journey, you find that you start looking like a brave warrior, ready for battle. Psalm 116:8-9 (NASB) says, "For You have rescued my soul from death, My eyes from tears, My feet from stumbling. I shall walk before the LORD in the land of the living." How good it is to be seen as a soldier waiting for battle rather than an invalid lying helpless on the sidewalk! When God equips you, He equips you for success. Victory is on the horizon!

13. Have you ever suffered from depression?

Have you ever suffered from depression, or known a loved one who has? The alarming statistics for this age is that one in every two people is affected by depression. It is either that they are depressed themselves or know someone close to them who has depression. It is very hard to understand this mental condition and even harder to treat it. People who are depressed try to hide behind a mask as far as possible. I am not talking about those times when things are not going well and you feel down. It is when your mental capacities are severely impacted and you are not in a position to function as normal.

Having lived with a person who suffered from clinical depression for seven years, gave me first-hand experience on this mental ailment. This debilitating illness is like a mist that slowly creeps up on you. It impacts all aspects of a person's life, not just their mental faculties. When you are depressed you feel God has forsaken you. You try to pray but it seems like your prayers fall on deaf ears, like it felt for me. The truth of the matter is that those who are clinically depressed do need medical help as well as the support and understanding of family members. You cannot go on this journey on your own, without the help of others and think that you will come out of it. Swallow your pride, get a reality check and do something!

Through His Eyes -

Psalm 73 describes the lament of the soul of one who does the good thing but goes through such agony of the heart. It seems like the wicked prosper and the innocent suffer and even God appears to be distant from them. But this is not so; it only *seems* that way. God has been faithful, is faithful and will remain faithful to those who follow Him earnestly. Psalm 73:21-28 (NIV) says, "When my heart was grieved and my spirit embittered, I was senseless and ignorant; I was a brute beast before you. Yet I am always with you; you hold me by my right hand. You guide me with your counsel, and afterward you will take me into glory. Whom have I in heaven but you? And earth has nothing I desire besides you. My flesh and my heart may fail, but God is the strength of my heart and my portion forever. Those who are far from you will perish; you destroy all who are unfaithful to you. But as for me, it is good to be near God. I have made the Sovereign Lord my refuge; I will tell of all your deeds." *Indeed, in my case, God is faithful and although it didn't happen the way I anticipated, God did come through for me.* I believe He can do the same for you, if you let Him.

We do not need to journey alone through a storm; help is available. We just need to be willing to reach out and receive that help. I would strongly urge you to get help from a reputable doctor and a counselor. I have also found that seeking spiritual counsel and support from a wise pastor or spiritually mature friend has helped me tremendously. Counselling has helped me clarify many aspects of doubt in my mind. We can ponder so much about an issue and pursue a certain direction, only to find that it is the wrong direction. Professional and spiritual help is vitally important in guiding you towards the light. Never think you know it all; that is pride and we know that pride goes before a fall. Do the right thing and find something profitable for yourself and your loved one to get out of that depression.

14. Hope for the hopeless

Have you ever felt like you were totally abandoned? Did you find yourself left to fend for yourself in a vast sea of rough waves? Take heart, you are not the only one.

Through His Eyes -

When living with someone with severe depression, you do sometimes feel like the odds are stacked up against you. When you find yourself in such a situation, hope is the last word on your mind. You often wonder if it is remotely possible to think that way.

When stressed, we tend to pop some pills in our mouth and magically in a short period, we feel much better. But can medication solve all our problems? Many people seem to think so yet when the problem has underlying issues, generally the symptoms are treated rather than the cause. Unless we look at the cause, the treatment we do take is only a band aid over a bleeding cut. This is very often the case with sicknesses that cannot be seen directly like mental health disorders. We have to get to the root of the problem to treat the illness correctly.

So how can you have hope in a situation that appears hopeless? We have the God of the universe, the One who made even our tiny planet amidst the great galaxies, who offers us hope. He knows our human frailty and struggles with life. That is why He sent His only Son, the Lord Jesus Christ, to walk this earth as a man and experience all the frailty of man. The Lord Jesus Christ came to this world to redeem our life and give us the gift of eternal life. Even though you may feel that all is lost and your ship is sinking, you have *hope*!

You are never ever abandoned by your Maker. John 3:16-17 (NIV) says, "For God so loved the world that He gave His one and only Son, that everyone who believes in Him shall not perish but have eternal life. For God did not send His Son into the world to condemn the world, but to save the world through Him." We have the hope that we will not perish and will live with Him forever!

It doesn't matter what your heart tells you, look at the Word of God and draw strength from it. Lamentations 3:24 (NASB) says, "'The Lord is my portion,' says my soul, 'Therefore I have hope in Him!'" What we think directly influences our mind and our actions because how we think is how we will respond to situations. Very often what we *feel* affects the way we think. If you think positive things about your situation and focus on plans for your future, you begin to anticipate good outcomes.

Someone said we *become* what we think. Romans 8:5-6 (NIV) says, "Those who live according to the flesh set their minds on the things of the flesh; but those who live according to the Spirit set their minds on the things of the Spirit. The mind of the flesh is death, but the mind of the Spirit is life and peace." Therefore, I urge you to think life and look up to the Life Giver.

Sometimes you may be doing so well and then things come crashing down. You try to give all the support you can to your loved one and it seems they are recovering but then out of the blues, your loved one relapses and you are shattered. Psalm 42 recounts the experience of King David as his heart anguished over the troubles he found himself in. Psalm 42:1-5 (NIV) says, "My soul thirsts for God, for the living God. When can I go and meet with God? My tears have been my food day and night, while people say to me all day long, 'Where is your God?' These things I remember as I pour out my soul: how I used to go to the house of God under the protection of the Mighty One with shouts of joy and praise among the festive throng. Why, my soul, are you downcast? Why so disturbed within me? Put your hope in God, for I will yet praise him, my Saviour and my God." This Psalm, like so many related verses in the Bible, point us to the only true source of consolation. We know that our Lord Jesus Christ who knew exactly what it is to be man and what we feel through the valley experiences, is the only one qualified to give us hope.

We have a divine consolation that we will receive deliverance. Psalm 41:1-3 (NIV) says, "Blessed are those who have regard for the weak; the Lord delivers them in times of trouble. The Lord protects and preserves them— they are counted among the blessed in the land— he does not give them over to the desire of their foes. The Lord sustains them on their sickbed and restores them from their bed of illness." So, no matter what the ups and downs entail in our lives, we have the assurance that the God in whom we trust is faithful and

He *will* deliver us from our adverse situations. There is hope for the hopeless!

15. Light at the end of the tunnel

It was a very long road and I took my wife to the best medical team I could afford. I also sought the help of prayer warriors. It is vitally important that when we are in our darkest moments, we should focus our energies on the hope of one day seeing the light shining through. I know that although she was not functioning well, deep down inside her soul, my severely depressed wife was determined to fight and get out of her situation. When one mighty man of God prayed for her, there was a difference. That night she slept like a baby, after a very long time.

There were several things we did to help my wife through this long-drawn battle of depression. As soon as I saw that she was responding, we pursued pathways she could undertake. We were finally able to help her get out of her room, get out into the garden and slowly get out of the house. She hesitantly went for group therapy at an AA affiliated mental health organization. Later she took an online behaviour therapy course. When she had regained sufficient confidence, she was able to drive herself and went for regular one-on-one counselling sessions with the church counsellor. We started to notice a change in her; light was beginning to shine through those once vacant eyes.

We know that if you want something to happen, you sometimes have to wait in expectation. Just like a pregnant woman, you wait for the day she will come to full term when you will see the child she is carrying in her womb. The expectation that burns within us is the flame that ignites the anticipated outcome. Gradually my wife started seeing some of her old friends. It was not easy and very often she would get up from a conversation and say she has had enough, she needs to go. We all respected that place she was in and were carful not to overstimulate her brain. *I saw that she was taking baby steps but thank God, they were in the right direction.* A word of caution: as people looking in from the outside, we must be careful not to assume things. Everyone is different and each person has their own threshold. I learnt that very quickly!

I must stress how important it is to work with all stakeholders in the interest of the person suffering from depression. We worked closely with our doctor and the rest of the medical team throughout her ailing years. When we saw the remarkable progress she was finally making, it was time to reclaim her old self. At this stage, I must re-emphasise the work of the team because the last thing you want happening is for the sufferer to experience a relapse. With all the stakeholders involved, my wife finally began the journey of weaning off some of her strong drugs. I noticed she was less moody and I was able to have a decent conversation with her. It felt like an eternity but we were finally beginning to see some light at the end of the tunnel.

It was another great step forward when my wife started doing volunteer work. Although she had qualified to help people with a disability, she was not ready to take on the responsibility of a job, even if it was part time. We knew that we had to tread very cautiously because she was very vulnerable. Even though she was willing, her mind was still healing. She was getting out of the house and that was a positive sign. She was much calmer and started taking a proactive role around the house and the garden. She started driving to the local grocery store. These may seem like trivial things but for us it was a big thing because for years she refused to go out and now she was doing it on her own. *I can't describe the feeling, but it was such a great relief to be experiencing 'normal' again.*

There *is* a light at the end of the tunnel even though you may not be able to see it. When a train is going through a long tunnel, the occupants don't go into panic attack, jump off their seats and scramble to the exit to bail out. They know that it is just a small part of their journey that they have to be in that tunnel. Likewise, to those who are experiencing depression or are journeying with a loved one through it, please understand the reality; you are in the tunnel phase of your journey.

It is a sad truth that some people, for various reasons, bail out of life and others bury their head into the ground like the ostrich and are never able to come through the journey. Remember, you are never alone and you do not have to face that demon of depression all by yourself. There are so many willing hands to help you make it through. Just like that marathon runner who falls at the end of the race, his comrades are there to support him. They lift him up and drag him to the finish line, *if* he allows them to do so.

Most importantly, I have found that in the seven years of prolonged agony that my family and I experienced with my beloved wife, I was not alone. Very often I felt abandoned but that was far from the case because it was just my head and my heart fighting each other. My greatest strength came from the One who sustained me through this long ordeal. Trusting in God's unfailing love will see you through anything, no matter how looming the challenge may be. King David experienced calamity upon calamity till his soul was stretched to the limit. Yet he always looked up to God. In some psalms it seemed like he was fighting with God; kicking and screaming like a child having a tantrum. Through his life's journey, in good times and in bad times, he never failed to look up to God and that is probably why he is fondly referred to as a man after God's own heart. (1 Samuel 13:14 and Acts 13:22)

What do we do when we are in the tunnel? We can learn valuable lessons from those who had many tunnel experiences and came through it successfully. Here is a classic lament of the soul: Psalm 143:6-9 (NIV) "I spread out my hands to you; I thirst for you like a parched land. Answer me quickly, Lord; my spirit fails. Do not hide your face from me or I will be like those who go down to the pit. Let the morning bring me word of your unfailing love, for I have put my trust in you. Show me the way I should go, for to you I entrust my life. Rescue me from my enemies, Lord, for I hide myself in you." This rescue station is open to anyone at any time. What an assurance that is, especially for someone who is in sinking sand!

There is a big difference between knowing what to do and actually doing it. Having in your bookshelf a manual to fix a leaking tap is not going to be of any use unless you get it out and follow the instructions. If you do nothing, you will be in deep water, simple as that! Psalm 143:10-12 (NIV) continues, "Teach me to do your will, for you are my God; may your good Spirit lead me on level ground. For your name's sake, LORD, preserve my life; in your righteousness, bring me out of trouble. In your unfailing love, silence my enemies; destroy all my foes, for I am your servant." Our Lord is our protector and we can run to Him to shield us from whatever or whoever we are facing. When we go to Him, we know with all certainty that He will lift us out of our troubles and place us on higher ground. He is our deliverer and He will never abandon us. Therefore, we have the assurance that the light will break through the darkest time of our life and we will walk in the brightness of the future God has in store for us.

16. Changing adversity into advantage

When the storm clouds are darkening your environment and threatening to bring total destruction your way, that is exactly the time to focus on what lies ahead. This time calls for forward thinking; you see what is coming and you carefully strategize how you are going to ride out that storm. One of the greatest scriptures my wife and I took comfort from is Psalm 23. The Lord is indeed our Shepherd and He will lead us to lush green pastures (verse 2) for our souls to be refueled and refreshed. If you truly believe that this is what God has planned for your life, you can face the adversity with courage and move with the boldness of a lion.

Life calls for courage and those who want to win the battle need to put on their battle clothes and make sure their armour is in good shape. Joshua 1:8-9 (NASB) says, "This book of the law shall not depart from your mouth, but you shall meditate on it day and night, so that you may be careful to do according to all that is written in it; for then you will make your way prosperous, and then you will have success. Have I not commanded you? Be strong and courageous. Do not be afraid; do not be discouraged, for the Lord your God will be with you wherever you go." So, if you know your commander in chief is strong and powerful, you *know* you are on the winning side.

Anyone who goes into battle knows that they have to look forward all the time. If they are constantly looking back, they risk being shot. We need to forget the past and avoid the tendency to think of what should have or could have been the situation if only we had done whatever... Isaiah 43:18-19 (NASB) says, "Do not call to mind the former things, Or ponder things of the past. Behold, I will do something new, Now it will spring forth; Will you not be aware of it? I will even make a roadway in the wilderness, Rivers in the desert."

Therefore, in the face of adversity we need to run with determination, focusing on the great things God has in store for us. This requires practice for some people and like the men conscripted for army training, we need to get in line and follow the path set before us.

For us not to let depression and discouragement pull us down, we need to position ourselves correctly. We have to believe the positive and more importantly, *speak* out the positive. Our thoughts propel us into actions. It is like an incubator; the thoughts we think sit there in our brain and germinate. So be careful what you think; there is enough power to produce either death or life. Colossians 3:2 (NASB) says, "Set your mind on the things above, not on the things that are on earth." I had to constantly remind myself of this principle because by nature I tend to be a worry bag. I had to train my mind to dwell on the positive because I am more inclined to focus on the negative. But when you break this mindset, it is so liberating. It is like inhaling the breeze of fresh air when someone opens up the windows in a stuffy apartment.

Whatever the enemy throws at you, place it into God's hands and watch what happens next. As you put your full confidence in God to fight your battle for you, just rest in Him and see how He turns that adversity into advantage. Isaiah 41:10 (NIV) says, "So do not fear, for I am with you; do not be dismayed, for I am your God. I will strengthen you and help you; I will uphold you with my righteous right hand." So, when you have come to that place where you have done your part, just sit back and watch what God does next. You will be amazed and you might find that it will knock your socks off, like it did in my case. Nothing, absolutely nothing, is impossible with God.

17. Faith

When challenging times come, it challenges your faith. It is only in the furnace of life that we are able to develop an unswerving heart. When we come to the point where we can stand firm in our belief that God will see us through, His peace permeates our entire being. We realize that the battle belongs to the Lord and we can trust Him to see us through. *I heard many people talk about this peace but I had not found it.* It was like my head was being constantly dumped in a bucket of cold water by a bully. I was trying to be brave and strong in my own strength in the face of opposition.

Opposition will come our way anytime and anywhere. How we handle it is vital to the outcome. Psalm 27:1 & 3 (NIV) says, "The Lord is my light and my salvation – whom shall I fear? The Lord is the stronghold of my life – of whom shall I be afraid? Verse 3 -Though an army besiege me, my heart will not fear; though war break out against me, even then I will be confident." This is something I found to be true in my life all the time. Having my faith fixed on God and trusting Him at His word, has always seen me through, irrespective of how insurmountable the situation appeared. I shudder to think what I would have done or where I would have been if I didn't go to God in prayer when all the odds were stacked against me.

Through His Eyes -

The choice is yours how you respond to situations life throws at you. Imagine been wrongly accused and thrown into prison; what would you do? Many people would look for the best lawyer to sue their wrongdoers. Here is an example of a man who constantly received the harsh punishment of the law for doing something good. What did he do? In Romans 12:17-19 (NIV) Paul writes, "Do not repay anyone evil for evil. Be careful to do what is right in the eyes of everyone. If it is possible, as far as it depends on you, live at peace with everyone. Do not take revenge, my dear friends, but leave room for God's wrath, for it is written: 'It is mine to avenge; I will repay,' says the Lord." This is a not easy to comprehend but it is a valuable lesson to learn. We cannot always question what life sends our way but what we do with it is most important.

When things go wrong, like they sometimes do, we need that reassurance that we are going to make it through on the other side. This cannot be guaranteed by our own strength or limited understanding. We need something greater than ourselves to lean on, something that has stood the test of time. Psalm 27:13-14 (NASB) talks about David's experience when he was faced with storms in his life; he says, "I would have despaired unless I had believed that I would see the goodness of the Lord in the land of the living. Wait for the Lord; Be strong and let your heart take courage; Yes, wait for the Lord." So, don't despair, in God's time you will receive the answer you are waiting for.

Expectation is waiting eagerly for something to happen. We function best when we obey God and are doing the will of God. Did you know that our Heavenly Father doesn't expect us to do anything on our own; He expects us to rely on Him. When God works on something, the result is always a masterpiece. It is not about who you are or what you can or cannot do. When you are feeling down, you need to look *up*. Only when you look up to God, are you able to rise from your situation. Romans 8:24 (NIV) says, "For in this hope we were saved. But hope that is seen is no hope at all. Who hopes for what they already have?"

Endurance is that resolution that you will make it. Don't give up; be determined and look to God because He is the one who energizes us and makes us anew. Remember it is the Lord that gives us the strength. 2 Corinthians 5:17 says, "Therefore if any man be in Christ Jesus, he is a new creation: old things are passed away; behold all things are become new." It is only through God that we can break free of the bonds that hold us captive. God can take our brokenness and make us totally whole and new. You are God's masterpiece and He doesn't make junk. As I journeyed through my faith walk, this became more evident to me – I am a masterpiece in God's hand.

Knowing all about what God can do for us, we need to exercise our faith in Him and speak to our situation. Proverbs 18:21 (NIV) says, "The tongue has the power of life and death, and those who love it will eat its fruit."

Did you know that what you say is what you get? If you say 'I am so stressed out', your stress level will rise further. If you constantly say 'I am buggered', you will feel run down and buggered. God did not lead you on a journey of power for you to go back to living a powerless existence. Speak life and see how liberating it is to your entire being.

18. Habits

The path you walk becomes the road that you travel. The way we think about ourselves is so important because it becomes engrained in our mindset. Our thinking influences how we see ourselves and this leads to the decisions we make. Just like how some people have poor physical hygiene and we can see from a mile away and they stink, some people have bad mental hygiene. If you are thinking thoughts that are not good for you for e.g. I'm stupid, I can't do this and so on, these are negative thoughts that lead to 'stinking thinking'. By constantly dwelling on those negatives, you are actually sending negative messages to your brain. So, when you say you are feeling rotten, you have been feeding your brain 'junk food'.

Did you know that 'should have' thinking doesn't influence what *did* happen? Think as much as you want, you simply cannot change the past. When you dwell on negative things too long, you make yourself unhappy and this can escalate to a depressed state. When bad things happen, do you blame yourself? Instead of stinking thinking use logical reasoning to work through the situation. When you break the habit of using that stinking thinking, you are actually liberating yourself. You are breaking the strongholds in your mind and unshackling yourself. Think positive and you will get positive results!

There are some habits that directly affect people close to us. Worry is contagious; it leaves a dark cloud over today's sunshine. Ever tried driving a car and all the gears are stuck except the reverse gear? Worry is faith in reverse gear. Not only are you going backwards when you worry, you are blatantly disobeying God's command.

Don't you think that Father God knows what you need? He is more than able to provide for you. Proverbs 3:5-8 (NIV) says, "Trust in the LORD with all your heart and lean not on your own understanding; in all your ways submit to him, and he will make your paths straight. Do not be wise in your own eyes; fear the Lord and shun evil. This will bring health to your body and nourishment to your bones." Do the right thing!

We can win the battle on worry by putting our full trust in our Heavenly Father. *I have found that when I tried to work things out my own way, I always fell flat on my face.* You need to come to the realization where you rely totally on what the Word of God says. Matthew 6:33-34 (NIV) says, "But seek first His kingdom and His righteousness, and all these things will be given to you as well. Therefore, do not worry about tomorrow, for tomorrow will worry about itself. Each day has enough trouble of its own." Once you set you focus right and seek God first, you will be amazed, just like me, on how He will take care of those things that are worrying you.

Do you realize that when you worry about tomorrow, you are draining yourself of your strength for today? It steals strength from the next day and robs you of your joy. Worry will sabotage the blessing that God has in store for you. He certainly has great things in store for us. You need to slay those giants that are keeping you away from experiencing an abundant life.

Habits that are counter-productive to our well-being need to be dealt with, not pushed under the carpet. Don't make excuses for those nasty habits; instead do something about them now. Nobody wants to walk around with a leech attached to their skin; it drains the life blood out of you. So, rip out that faulty mindset and replace it with a life-giving source. You will be so liberated, energized and refueled for the future!

19. Share it!

When you think that all is lost and there is nothing to look forward to in life, you fall to your knees in defeat. However, the greatest test requires the greatest faith to produce the greatest reward. When you are at your weakest and all your efforts have failed, you cry to God to please take over. Then wait to see what He does next. My wife, who was diagnosed with chronic depression for seven years, supernaturally was raised from her state of drugged stupor and walked from the valley to the mountain. *I never dreamt that her full recovery will become a reality to such remarkable proportions.*

When you have been to hell and back, you can't keep it to yourself. You simply have to share it! I prayed for the day to come when I would know what it feels like to live in a normal household. God is faithful and His promises are dependable. We may not operate on His time frame but it doesn't mean He has abandoned us. In His time, He makes all things beautiful. Psalm 40:5 (NIV) says,

"Many, Lord my God, are the wonders You have done, the things You planned for us. None can compare with You; were I to speak and tell of Your deeds, they would be too many to declare."

What a great God we have and what a great Saviour we serve. *I am eternally grateful to God for restoring my life and giving me back my dearest friend and life partner.* God is faithful; we just have to trust Him wholeheartedly! It doesn't matter how big your storm is or how long it rages on, when you call out to God, like I did, you can ride out your storm with Him by your side. Just put your full trust in Him and don't look back. The sun will shine again and you will be smiling.

When God does a work in your life, He does a complete work. There is healing, restoration and empowerment. He makes you brand new again. He is more than we can ever imagine. Ephesians 3:20-21(NASB) has become a reality in our lives. "Now to Him who is able to do exceedingly abundantly above all that we ask or think, according to the power that works in us, to Him be glory in the church by Christ Jesus to all generations, forever and ever. Amen."

So, much to my amazement, the journey of depression that my beloved wife travelled through has taken on a new turn. When God healed and restored her, He also healed and restored our family. What I have discovered is that my faith in Him was tested, refined and restored to a far greater measure than I ever anticipated. *I have likewise gone on my own journey of learning to depend on God for every little detail of my life. It was not easy and I was not very teachable at first, but the circumstances that brought me to my knees were the very ones that taught me the biggest lessons in life.*

20. Concluding remarks

This book is dedicated to my children and their children. I want them to understand what it is like living with and supporting a person with depression. *My prayer is that people who find themselves in a similar situation will read my story on living with a person with depression and draw strength from my journey. No matter how dark the path may be, remember there is always light at the end of the tunnel.*

My experience has taught me that you are never alone, even though at times you may feel so lonely and dejected. I have drawn from the timeless book that has changed the destiny of countless people's lives. You too can change the course you are travelling by seeking the right 'road map' for your journey in life.

Another valuable lesson I wish to share is that in all things, both good and bad, ultimately God is glorified. This may not make sense to some of you, but with time, we see that everything that happens in our lives shapes us to be the person we become. Those great people I mentioned who had depression went through long, dark journeys that molded their character and influenced their thought life. What we think is definitely what we become. If we think Kingdom Living, we get to live like a Royal Priesthood. ◊

21. About the Author

Linda Pearl Ramnath is the author of the following books:

1. You Don't Have To Settle For Second Best! A Life Of Hope, Courage And Determination
ISBN – Softcover: 978-1-4931-3410-6
ISBN – E-book: 1493134108

2. SOUL FOOD – Renew Your Mind!
ISBN – Softcover: 978-0-9925761-0-3
ISBN – E-book: 9781493134090

3. SOUL FOOD – Restore Your Soul!
ISBN – Softcover: 978-0-9925761-1-0
ISBN – E-book: 9781311074973

4. Through His Eyes – What We Did To Overcome Depression
ISBN – Softcover: 978-0-9925761-2-7
ISBN – E-book: 978-1-3794730-3-1

She is one of the co-authors of **Authors For Christ** in the following book:

5. Stories of Hope – Powerful Testimonies of Encouragement
ISBN – 13: 978-1535076159
ISBN – 10: 1535076151

6. Let Hope Arise: Powerful Testimonies of Hope and Encouragement
ISBN – 13: 978-1540884237
ISBN – 10: 1540884236

Linda Pearl Ramnath is the blogger on this website:
www.donotsettleforsecondbest.com

To obtain books written by this author, go to Amazon, Barnes and Noble, Smashwords or any other leading bookseller. Books available in print form and digital versions.

Search online for Linda Pearl Ramnath:

Amazon, Xlibris, Google, Smashwords, Twitter, LinkedIn

****

Notes

www.ingramcontent.com/pod-product-compliance
Lightning Source LLC
Chambersburg PA
CBHW071312040426
42444CB00009B/1989